Blue Banner Biography

David Ortiz

Joanne Mattern

P.O. Box 196
Hockessin, Delaware 19707
Visit us on the web: www.mitchelllane.com
Comments? email us: mitchelllane@mitchelllane.com

Mitchell Lane PUBLISHERS

Printing   2   3   4   5   6   7   8   9

Blue Banner Biographies

Akon	Alan Jackson	Alicia Keys
Allen Iverson	Ashanti	Ashlee Simpson
Ashton Kutcher	Avril Lavigne	Bernie Mac
Beyoncé	Bow Wow	Britney Spears
Carrie Underwood	Chris Brown	Chris Daughtry
Christina Aguilera	Christopher Paul Curtis	Ciara
Clay Aiken	Condoleezza Rice	Daniel Radcliffe
David Ortiz	Derek Jeter	Eminem
Eve	Fergie (Stacy Ferguson)	50 Cent
Gwen Stefani	Ice Cube	Jamie Foxx
Ja Rule	Jay-Z	Jennifer Lopez
Jessica Simpson	J. K. Rowling	Johnny Depp
JoJo	Justin Berfield	Justin Timberlake
Kate Hudson	Keith Urban	Kelly Clarkson
Kenny Chesney	Lance Armstrong	Lindsay Lohan
Mariah Carey	Mario	Mary J. Blige
Mary-Kate and Ashley Olsen	Michael Jackson	Miguel Tejada
Missy Elliott	Nancy Pelosi	Nelly
Orlando Bloom	P. Diddy	Paris Hilton
Peyton Manning	Queen Latifah	Ron Howard
Rudy Giuliani	Sally Field	Selena
Shakira	Shirley Temple	Tim McGraw
Usher	Zac Efron	

Library of Congress Cataloging-in-Publication Data
Mattern, Joanne, 1963-
  David Ortiz / by Joanne Mattern.
    p. cm. — (Blue banner biographies)
  Includes bibliographical references and index.
  ISBN-13: 978-1-58415-620-8 (library bound)
  1. Ortiz, David, 1975- —Juvenile literature. 2. Baseball players—Dominican Republic—Biography—Juvenile literature. I. Title.
  GV865.O78M37 2008
  796.357092—dc22
  [B]
                                                                        2007019794

ABOUT THE AUTHOR: Joanne Mattern is the author of more than 200 nonfiction books for children, including *Brian McBride*, *Peyton Manning*, and *Miguel Tejada* for Mitchell Lane Publishers. Along with biographies, she has written extensively about animals, nature, history, sports, and foreign cultures. She lives near New York City with her husband and three young daughters.

PHOTO CREDITS: Cover—Jed Jacobsohn/Getty Images; p. 4—Craig Ambrosio/Getty Images; p. 7—Ezra Shaw/Getty Images; p. 10—Timothy Clary/Getty Images; p. 11—Dave Kaup/Getty Images; p. 13—David Maxwell/Getty Images; pp. 15, 21, 29—Al Bello/Getty Images; p. 18—Jim McIsaac/Getty Images; pp. 23, 25—Rich Pilling/Getty Images; p. 27—Elsa/Getty Images; p. 28—Heart Care Dominicana foundation/Getty Images

Blue Banner Biography

David Ortiz is one of baseball's most powerful hitters. He started his major-league career in 1997, playing first base for the Minnesota Twins. By the end of 2002, he would be a free agent.

The Player
Nobody Wanted

At the end of 2002, David Ortiz was struggling. His team, the Minnesota Twins, had seen many ups and downs over the last four seasons—and so had Ortiz. The first baseman had missed a lot of games because of injuries. The Twins had not played well enough to make it to the playoffs.

Earlier in the season, it looked as if 2002 would be different. Ortiz hit 20 home runs, and the Twins won 94 games. The team made it to the division playoffs and beat the Oakland Athletics. They were riding high, but Ortiz was not. He batted only .231 during the series.

The Twins knew they faced a tough team when they went up against the Anaheim Angels in the American League Championship Series. Although Ortiz hit a respectable .312 and drove in several runs, it wasn't enough. Anaheim took the series four games to one. The Twins would not be going to the World Series that year.

As the Twins management looked forward to 2003, they had some big decisions to make. One of them was whether to keep David Ortiz. They were paying him a lot of money, and they weren't sure he was worth the price. He'd had too many injuries, too many batting slumps. The Twins decided to trade him. "He just wasn't getting it done here," said Minnesota's general manager, Terry Ryan.

Both Ortiz and Ryan thought that another team would be eager to sign the powerful player, but nobody was interested. "Not one team made an offer," Ryan said.

Ortiz was upset and angry. He felt the Twins didn't respect him, and now it seemed no other team respected him either. He thought about playing in Japan or Mexico instead of for Major League Baseball.

> Ortiz was. . . angry. He thought about playing in Japan or Mexico instead of for Major League Baseball.

In December 2002, the Twins gave up. They made Ortiz a free agent, meaning he would be free to sign with any club that would take him. Soon afterward, the Boston Red Sox offered him a contract. Ortiz would be taking a pay cut, but he didn't care. He was just happy to be playing ball.

It didn't take long before David Ortiz showed everyone that he truly was a great player. He slammed homers. He drove in runs. Best of all, he gave the Red Sox a chance to break the fabled Curse of the Bambino.

In 1919, the Red Sox had traded a young Babe Ruth, whose nickname was the Bambino, to the New York

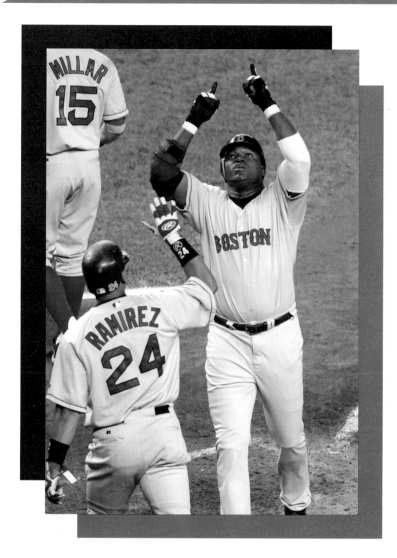

It's high fives between David and Red Sox teammate Manny Ramirez after David hits a home run against the New York Yankees. The Red Sox and Yankees have been archrivals for generations.

Yankees. His trade was one of the worst decisions in baseball history. Babe Ruth went on to lead the Yankees to many championships. He set many records and became one of the best players ever. Fans believed that when Boston traded the Bambino, they brought down a curse that would never let them win a World Series. Indeed, they hadn't won since 1918.

When David Ortiz came to town, their luck seemed to change.

Growing Up with Baseball

David Americo Ortiz Arias was born on November 18, 1975, in Santo Domingo, the capital city of the Dominican Republic. His father was Enrique "Leo" Ortiz and his mother was Angela Rosa Arias. Like many Latinos, David used his mother's name as his last name. He would not be called David Ortiz until he was an adult.

The family would soon grow to include four sisters for David. They did not have a lot of money, but there was a lot of love. David was a happy child. He had fun with his family and loved to play with his friends in the neighborhood.

David grew up playing baseball, which is very popular in the Dominican Republic. He had another reason to love the sport. It was something he could share with his father, who played in several professional baseball leagues.

David enjoyed playing other sports too, including soccer and basketball. By the time he was a teenager, he was big and strong. He would grow to be six feet, four inches tall and weigh more than 200 pounds. Everyone could see he would be a power hitter when he stepped up to the plate to bat.

At Estudia Espallat High School in Santo Domingo, David played both baseball and basketball. He was the best player on the basketball team. No one could stop him from scoring, and he dreamed of playing basketball professionally.

Before he graduated, David realized he was not good enough to be a professional basketball player. His father agreed and encouraged him to focus on baseball. David clearly had the skills to play in the major leagues. He stayed relaxed at the plate, and he could place the ball anywhere in the field. Scouts from the Seattle Mariners major league team had their eye on David. They decided that this young slugger had what it took. Just ten days after his seventeenth birthday, the Mariners signed him to a minor league contract. David was on his way.

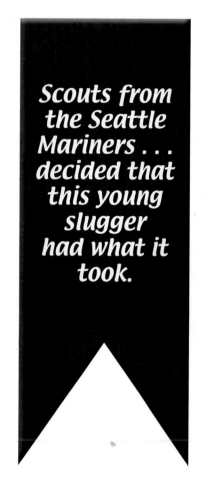

Scouts from the Seattle Mariners . . . decided that this young slugger had what it took.

David's professional baseball career started in the Dominican Republic, where the Mariners had a minor league team. David played for the team in the summer of 1993. He did well, batting .264 with 35 extra-base hits in 61 games.

In 1994, nineteen-year-old David was ready to go to the United States. The Mariners sent the left-handed hitter to their minor league team in Peoria, Illinois.

Living the United States was a big change for David. So was playing for a U.S. team. He had a hard time at first.

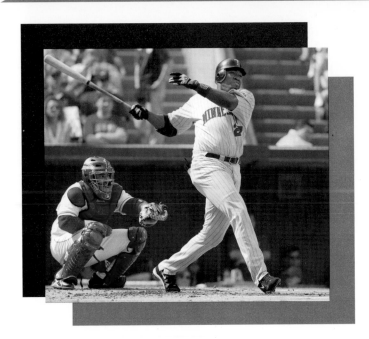

David hits a double during game five of the 2002 American League Championship Series between the Minnesota Twins and the Anaheim Angels. The Angels would win the series 4 games to 1, keeping the Twins out of the World Series for yet another year.

David had to learn to speak English and get used to life in a new country. He also missed his family back home. He managed to overcome these obstacles because he loved baseball so much. He did everything he could to be a great player.

During his first season in Peoria, David batted only .246. However, he showed everyone that he was a great fielder and first baseman. In 1995, he did much better at the plate. His batting average shot up to a terrific .332, and from June to July he had a nineteen-game hitting streak. He also led the league in doubles and RBIs, or runs batted in, and in fielding, with a .989 percentage.

The year 1996 found David in Wisconsin. His new team was the Wisconsin Timber Rattlers of the Class A Midwest League. David set the Timber Rattlers on fire and became one of the Mariners' rising stars. In 129 games that season, his batting average was .322. His statistics included 34 doubles, 2 triples, 18 home runs, and 93 RBIs.David was voted one of

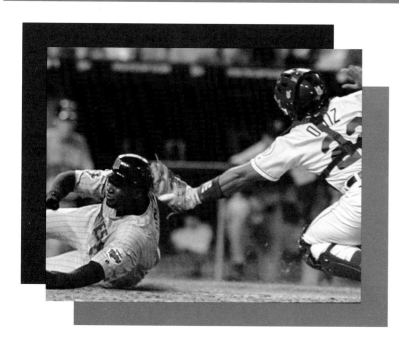

David Ortiz is tagged out by Hector Ortiz during a game in 2001 against the Kansas City Royals.

the Midwest League's All-Stars, and the magazine *Baseball America* voted him as the league's Most Exciting Player.

Another great thing happened while David was in Wisconsin. He met a local girl named Tiffany Brick. The couple soon got married. In 1997, their daughter Yessica was born.

In September 1996, David was at home in the Dominican Republic when he got some interesting news. The Mariners had traded him to the Minnesota Twins. David was sorry that he would not continue to play for the Mariners. However, he knew moving to the Twins could be a great opportunity when he advanced to the major leagues. David usually played first base, and he also served as the team's designated hitter. The Mariners already had strong players for these jobs, but the Twins did not. David told the Twins he was ready to play for them. He also asked them to call him by a new name. From then on, he would be David Ortiz.

Success and Disappointment

David Ortiz started his career with the Twins with their Class A minor league team, the Fort Myers Miracle. During April and May 1997, the team could hardly believe how good he was. He hit safely in his first 11 games, achieving a .432 batting average. In May, the Twins named him the organization's Minor League Player of the Month. In June, they promoted him to the next level, Class AA. He moved from the AA team to the AAA team in July. Finally, in September, Ortiz got the call he was waiting for. He was invited to join the major league Twins for the rest of the season.

Ortiz had a great time in his first major league games. He ended the season with a .327 average over 15 games. He was invited back to the Twins for spring training. When the team's manager, Tom Kelly, made up his roster for the 1998 season, Ortiz was on the team.

The season started well, with Ortiz going on a seven-game hitting streak in April. Then disaster struck. Ortiz broke his right wrist. He could not play again until June.

David leads the Twins to victory with this game-winning RBI against the Cleveland Indians in September 2000. He had worked hard in the minor leagues before he finally gained a permanent spot in the majors that year.

When he returned, he picked up where he'd left off. Even though he only played 86 games that season, he finished with 46 RBIs and 9 home runs. His batting average was .277, making him one of the best rookies in the American League.

Ortiz had high hopes when the 1999 season started, but he did not do well in spring training. Instead of starting the season at first base for the Twins, he was sent down to a minor league team called the Salt Lake Stingers. Ortiz had a great season with the Stingers. He hit 30 home runs and led the league in RBIs. However, the Twins were not impressed.

Ortiz was angry and disappointed at being stuck in the minor leagues that season, but the Twins felt he needed to learn to be a better fielder. He also needed to be more careful at the plate and not swing at every pitch. When they called him up to play a few games with the Twins in September, Ortiz did not get on base in 20 at-bats. He struck out 12 times.

Ortiz worked hard to get better. After the 1999 season, he went home as usual to the Dominican Republic. There he played in the Dominican winter league, where he finished first in RBIs and second in batting and home runs.

He did so well in spring training that he was chosen to be on the Twins' major league roster when the season started.

Ortiz was confident that 2000 would be a great season. He did so well in spring training that he was chosen to be on the Twins' major league roster when the season started. He split the season between two positions—first baseman and designated hitter. The designated hitter's only job is to hit. He takes the place of a weak-hitting player, or the pitcher, when it is that player's turn to bat.

Indeed, the season was great. Ortiz finished with a .282 average and set career highs with 117 hits, 36 doubles, 10 home runs, and 63 RBIs. He also was a solid player in the field, making only one error all season. Despite the team's efforts, the Twins won only 69 games. Still, Ortiz had a good time. Always smiling and joking, he was popular with fans and with his teammates.

Although he now lives in the United States, David was proud to play for his homeland, the Dominican Republic, in the 2006 World Baseball Classic. He routinely plays for his homeland during Major League Baseball's off-season.

The Twins were a much better team in 2001. They won 85 games and led the American League's central division for part of the season. However, Ortiz did not shine. He broke his wrist again in May and needed surgery. When he rejoined the team in July, his wrist continued to bother him, and he did not get many hits. Only after a lot of work with batting coach Scott Ulger and assistant manager Paul Molitor did Ortiz get his old swing back. He ended the season with 18 home runs and 48 RBIs, but his average was a low .234.

Ortiz tried not to let his difficulties get him down. "Everybody goes through some tough times in their life, no matter what you do," he told *Sports Illustrated*.

Ortiz and his family did have one bright spot during 2001. That year, his second daughter, Alexandra, was born. However, David was about to face the most difficult time of his life.

Tragedy Strikes

*A*fter the 2001 season, Ortiz went back to the Dominican Republic. He spent the next few months visiting friends and family and playing baseball. Then, on January 1, 2002, he received devastating news. His mother had just been in a bad car accident.

Ortiz rushed to the scene of the crash, but he was too late. "I was there eight minutes after it happened, and she was dead already," he later told a reporter for *Sports Illustrated*.

The death of Angela Rosa Arias was a terrible blow for David. He had always called himself his mom's baby boy. "She was one of the best mothers ever," he told *Sports Illustrated*. "She was pretty much my everything. It's tough, man. I come from a poor family, but I had a good education and a good home. That counts for everything. My mom, she wasn't like a baseball mother who knew everything about the game. She just wanted me to be happy with what I was doing." Ortiz honored his mother by getting a large tattoo of her on his right arm.

Losing his mother changed his feelings about baseball. "I don't worry about baseball," Ortiz said. "I don't feel like

I put any pressure on myself when I'm playing baseball. Not after that." He told *Baseball Digest* that after his mother's death, "I have to be the stronger person. I don't think I have faced anything worse than that, anything more painful than that. That's why I see everything else in light and happiness."

His baseball family remained an important part of his life. His teammates and his new manager, Ron Gardenhire, gave Ortiz a lot of support and love when he showed up for spring training just a few weeks after Angela Rosa's death.

Ortiz didn't know it, but 2002 would be his last year with the Minnesota Twins. Despite a problem with his left knee early in the season and a long stretch of 43 games without a home run, Ortiz settled down during the second half of the season. He batted an incredible .419 after the All-Star break in July and helped his team to the top of the division. Ortiz ended the regular season with the best statistics of his career. He had 32 doubles, 20 home runs, and 75 RBIs. The Twins had a great year too. For the first time since 1991, they made it to

He batted an incredible .419 after the All-Star break in July and helped his team to the top of the division.

the playoffs. Then they beat the Oakland Athletics to win their division. The team's ride ended in the American League Championship Series. The Anaheim Angels beat the Twins four games to one, but Ortiz had done well, hitting .312 in the series.

David Ortiz of the Boston Red Sox and Pedro Martinez of the New York Mets talk before their game on June 27, 2006, at Fenway Park in Boston, Massachusetts. When Ortiz became a free agent in 2002, Martinez, who was playing for the Red Sox, found his friend a spot on the Boston team.

He was feeling good about himself. His contract scheduled him for a raise—to over two million dollars. But because of his uneven record, the Twins let him go. He was on his own.

Ortiz was upset. He doubted whether he was a good player after all. He talked to his friend Pedro Martinez, a star pitcher for the Boston Red Sox. Martinez believed in Ortiz, so he talked to the Red Sox and encouraged them to sign his friend. They offered Ortiz $1.25 million to play for one year, and Ortiz said yes. His career was about to go in a whole new direction.

The Road to the Championships

*T*he Boston Red Sox team was filled with strong and unusual personalities. Players such as Nomar Garciaparra, Manny Ramirez, and Pedro Martinez were hard to get along with. They often argued with each other and the news media. Would Ortiz be able to fit in with such difficult teammates?

David was up to the challenge. Even though the other players teased him at first because he was new, he managed to get along with everyone. Teammate Jason Varitek said, "He's just a joy to have on the team. He's going to have fun regardless of what's going on." David's high spirits helped his teammates get along with each other and play as a real team.

Although he liked his teammates, Ortiz at first was not happy in Boston. He was hired to play first base and be a designated hitter, but there were other players at these positions as well. He got so frustrated at his lack of playing time that he spoke to the Red Sox general manager, Theo Epstein. According to *Sports Illustrated*, Ortiz demanded that Epstein trade him. He told the manager, "I can't be sitting here watching this circus anymore. I know I can do better. Me just watching from the bench? I'm not that kind of guy." Epstein told Ortiz to give him a chance to move some players around. A few days later, he traded one of his players and made Ortiz the regular designated hitter. "We didn't know what we were getting," Epstein said about Ortiz. "We just let him be exactly what he is."

> *In 2003, he slammed 31 homers. The Red Sox won 95 games that season and made it into the playoffs.*

As soon as Ortiz had a chance to hit, his playing improved. In 2003, he slammed 31 homers. The Red Sox won 95 games that season and made it into the playoffs. After beating the Oakland Athletics in the division series, the Red Sox faced their longtime rivals, the New York Yankees, for the American League Championship.

Ortiz got the series off to a powerful start by hitting a home run that won the game for Boston, 5-2. However, the Yankees were not going to give up that easily. The series went to a full seven games. Although Ortiz hit a home run in game seven to give his team the lead, the Yankees came back to win the game and the series.

The Red Sox and their fans were very disappointed that they would not be going to the World Series. Even so, Ortiz did not give up. "I love Boston," he said. "I want to bring the fans a World Series title."

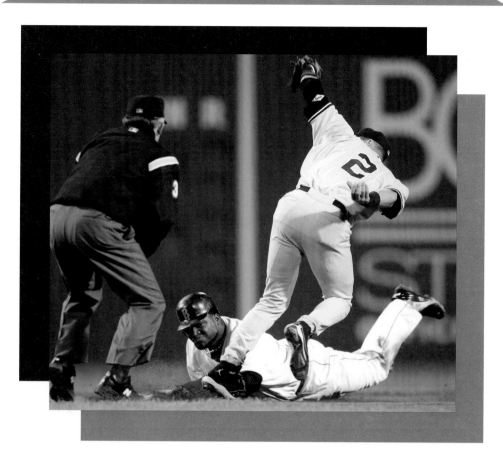

The Boston Red Sox and the New York Yankees would battle it out for the American League Championship Series in 2003 and 2004. Here, Ortiz tries to steal a base but is tagged out by Yankee Derek Jeter in the twelfth inning of game five of the 2004 series.

Ortiz believed in the Red Sox, and the Red Sox believed in him. Before the 2004 season, they gave him a new contract. He would be paid more than $12 million over the next two years.

Ortiz was happy to reward the Red Sox's faith in him. During 2004, he batted .301, hit 41 home runs and 47 doubles, and had 139 RBIs. For the first time, he was selected to join the All-Star team. Once again, the Red Sox made it to the playoffs.

The Red Sox beat the Anaheim Angels to win the division series, thanks to Ortiz's game-winning home run. Trouble lay ahead, though. Once again, the Red Sox faced the Yankees in the American League Championship Series. The Yankees were tough, and they easily won the first three games of the series. No team had ever won a seven-game series after being down three games to nothing.

The Red Sox decided to focus on winning just one game at a time. They won game four when Ortiz hit a home run in the twelfth inning. The next night, Ortiz hit a single that brought his teammate Johnny Damon home to win the game 5-4. The Red Sox also won game six.

Finally, it was winner-take-all in game seven. And the winner was the Red Sox! During the American League series, Ortiz hit three home runs and 11 RBIs. He was named the league's Most Valuable Player. Boston had done the impossible by coming back to win the series. Now it was time for the World Series.

The Red Sox faced the mighty St. Louis Cardinals in the 2004 World Series. Once again, Ortiz got his team going. In the first game, he had a home run and four RBIs. The Red Sox won the game 11-9. They went on to win the next three games and the title of World Series champions. It was the first time Boston had won the World Series since 1918. Fans declared the Curse of the Bambino was finally broken.

> *During the 2004 American League series, Ortiz hit three home runs and 11 RBIs.*

Ortiz fields the ball during game four of the 2004 World Series. The Red Sox would defeat the Cardinals in this game, 3-0. Although he is usually Boston's designated hitter, Ortiz is still a capable first baseman.

The city of Boston was thrilled. More than one million people came to the team's victory parade. Ortiz was one of the fans' favorite players. Dan Shaughnessy of *The Boston Globe* called David "an action superhero come to life." He had done what generations of great Red Sox players had not been able to do. Ortiz had helped the Red Sox win the World Series.

On Top of the World

*O*rtiz continued to shine in 2005. He became known as one of the best clutch hitters in baseball. A clutch hitter is a player who can get a hit when the team needs it most and the pressure is on. The Red Sox appreciated Ortiz's hitting abilities so much that they gave him a plaque that called him The Greatest Clutch Hitter in the History of the Boston Red Sox. "He loves coming up in the big spot," said Theo Epstein.

Ortiz gave credit for his hitting ability to being confident in himself and his team. "It's mostly confidence," he explained. "If you go up there thinking you might not get it done, you're out already. I know I'm going to hit you. And I have confidence all around me here. We don't care who's pitching."

In 2006, another hot year, Ortiz hit 54 homers to set a club record. Boston rewarded him with a new four-year contract worth $52 million.

Ortiz is called "Big Papi" or "Big Daddy" because of his powerful hits and his role as a team leader. He is one of the

David slams a home run in a game against the New York Yankees in April 2007. The Red Sox would go on to beat the Yankees that day, 7-4.

most popular players in the league, and also one of the most amazing. "It's beyond belief," teammate Kyle Snyder said of Ortiz's hitting ability. "It makes no sense."

Ortiz also has a wonderful family life. In 2004, Tiffany gave birth to a son, the couple's third child. They named him D'Angelo in honor of David's mother, Angela Rosa (the D is after David). David, his wife, and their three children live outside of Boston.

> *The workouts have made him thinner, fitter, and an even more powerful hitter.*

David has also become active in charity events in Boston. In October 2006, he played Wiffle Ball with more than 40 local children as part of Big Papi's Backyard Wiffle Ball Game. The game benefited Good Sports, a Boston-based organization that provides opportunities for disadvantaged children to get involved in sports. He has also donated at least $50,000 to Good Sports. He believes sports can be important to a child's future.

Ortiz knows that he needs to stay in good health to be a great player. Early in his career, wrist and knee injuries caused him a lot of problems. In 2006, he suffered what doctors thought was an irregular heartbeat after he pulled a muscle in his chest. Even though his heart was fine, Ortiz decided to start a new workout routine. He lifts weights and works with personal trainers. The workouts have made him thinner, fitter, and an even more powerful hitter. "It's good to be in good shape,"

David proudly wears his Red Sox colors as he warms up before a game in April 2007. He showed up for the season in excellent physical shape.

David gives generously to those in need. In December 2006, he donated $200,000 to Heart Care Dominicana. The money would be used to pay for heart surgery on children in need.

he said in early 2007. "It's good for my health. You have to take care of yourself, or it will catch up with you down the road."

Ortiz has long wanted to share his story with others. In 2007 he published his autobiography, *Big Papi: My Story of Big Dreams and Big Hits*, written with Tony Massaroti.

David Ortiz has come a long way from the player nobody wanted. He knows the secret to success is to never quit. "Life is a challenge," he told *Baseball Digest*. "There's things in life that are going to throw you into the ground, but if you learn how to get up, that means you are not a quitter. That's the best that a human being can have, never quit."

Ortiz plays in the 2006 All-Star Game in Pittsburgh, Pennslyvania.
Ortiz's American League team beat the National League team 3-2.

Major League Statistics

SEASON	TEAM	G	AB	R	H	2B	3B	HR	RBI	AVG
1997	Minnesota Twins	15	49	10	16	3	0	1	6	.327
1998	Minnesota Twins	86	278	47	77	20	0	9	46	.277
1999	Minnesota Twins	10	20	1	0	0	0	0	0	.000
2000	Minnesota Twins	130	415	59	117	36	1	10	63	.282
2001	Minnesota Twins	89	303	46	71	17	1	18	48	.234
2002	Minnesota Twins	125	412	52	112	32	1	20	75	.272
2003	Boston Red Sox	128	448	79	129	39	2	31	101	.288
2004	Boston Red Sox	150	582	94	175	47	3	41	139	.301
2005	Boston Red Sox	159	601	119	180	40	1	47	148	.300
2006	Boston Red Sox	151	558	115	160	29	2	54	137	.287
Career Totals		1043	3,666	622	1,037	263	11	231	763	.257

1975   David Americo Ortiz Arias is born in Santo Domingo, Dominican Republic, on November 18.

1992   David signs a minor league contract with the Seattle Mariners.

1994   David comes to the United States to play in the Mariners' minor leagues.

1996   David meets and marries Tiffany Brick. He is traded to the Minnesota Twins in December.

1997   Daughter Yessica is born.

1998   David breaks his wrist and misses two months of the season.

1999   David is sent down to the minor leagues.

2000   David returns to the major leagues.

2001   David breaks his wrist and again misses two months of the season; daughter Alexandra is born.

2002   David's mother is killed in a car accident on January 1; David is released by the Twins and is signed by the Boston Red Sox.

2004   David is named to the All-Star team; he leads the Red Sox to a World Series Championship; he is named the American League MVP; son D'Angelo is born.

2006   David sets a club record, hitting 54 home runs in a season; he signs a four-year, $52 million contract with the Red Sox.

2007   David comes to spring training fit and trim; he publishes his autobiography, *Big Papi: My Story of Big Dreams and Big Hits.*

For Young Readers

Keith, Ted. "Who's Your Papi?" *Sports Illustrated Kids*, June 2006, Vol. 18, Issue 6.

Savage, Jeff. *David Ortiz*. Minneapolis: Lerner Publications Company, 2006.

Smithwick, John. *Meet David Ortiz: Baseball's Top Slugger*. New York: PowerKids Press, 2007.

Works Consulted

Benjamin, Amalie. "David Ortiz: Baseball's Slugging Dominican." Baseball Digest, October 2005.

Browne, Ian. "Notes: Big Papi in Good Shape." Major League Baseball News, February 24, 2007, http://mlb.mlb.com/news/article. jsp?ymd=20070224&content_id=1814190&vkey=news_mlb&fext=. jsp&c_id=mlb

Guregian, Karen. "Papi Is Still Heart of Sox: Sleeker Ortiz Is a Healthy Sight," *Boston Herald*, March 11, 2007, http://redsox.bostonherald. com/redSox/view.bg?articleid=187764

Mellinger, Sam. "David Ortiz." *Baseball Digest*, December 2006, Vol. 65, Issue 10, pp. 46–48.

Rosenthal, Ken. "Ortiz Gets the Last Laugh." *Sporting News*, November 1, 2004, Vol. 228, Issue 44, p. 17.

Verducci, Tom. "Who's Your Papi?" *Sports Illustrated*, June 19, 2006, Vol. 104, Issue 25, pp. 42–47.

Web Sites

Boston Red Sox http://boston.redsox.mlb.com

ESPN.com, "David Ortiz"
    http://sports.espn.go.com/mlb/players/profile?statsId=5909

JockBio, "David Ortiz"
    http://www.jockbio.com/Bios/Ortiz/Ortiz_bio.html

INDEX